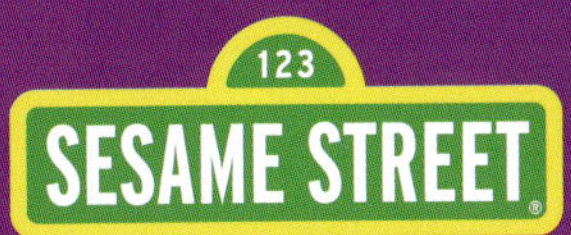

First Library Card with Big Bird

Whitney Sanderson

Lerner Publications ◆ Minneapolis

Discover six early milestones alongside your favorite *Sesame Street* friends! From visiting the dentist to getting a library card, this series helps young children feel prepared for new and exciting experiences that are a part of growing up.

Sincerely,
The Editors at Sesame Workshop

Table of Contents

Explore the Library!

A library is full of books! It's a fun place to explore and learn.

I'm reading my new book I got from the library!

Your Library Card

You can check out books with a library card. Checking out books means you borrow them and take them home for a while.

Me check out cookbooks and bring them home!

Your grown-up can help you get a library card. They'll introduce you to a librarian. A librarian works at a library!

Sometimes the librarian tells me about new books I might like!

The librarian might ask you questions such as what your name and address are. Your grown-up can help you answer. Then you will get a library card!

Elmo told the librarian that Elmo lives at 123 Sesame Street!

Librarians can also answer your questions and help you find a book you might be looking for.

Libraries have books about everything! Some libraries also have movies, games, and more.

I want to find a book about robots in space!

Libraries have computers too. Some even have activities such as story time and craft time for kids.

I go to story time with Papi every Saturday!

I get to borrow my library books for two weeks!

Library books have due dates. A due date is when you need to bring the book back to the library. When you're ready, the librarian will help you check out your books and tell you their due dates.

Take good care of the books you borrow so the next person can enjoy them too. You can pick out new books when you return the ones you read!

I can't wait to read my books and go back to my library!

Library Checkout Checklist

1. Choose the books you want to borrow.
2. Bring them to the library's front desk.
3. Give the librarian your library card to scan.
4. Go home and have fun reading your books!
5. Make sure you bring your books back by the due date.

Glossary

computers: machines you can use for typing, looking things up, and playing games

cookbooks: books of recipes for making food

librarian: a person who helps people at the library

library card: a card that lets you borrow books and other things from the library

Read More

Gabor, Nicole. *First Day of School with Ji-Young*. Minneapolis: Lerner Publications, 2026.

Press, J. P. *Libraries*. Minneapolis: Bearport, 2021.

StJohn, Amanda. *How to Check Out a Book*. Parker, CO: Child's World, 2023.

Photo Acknowledgments

Image credits: FatCamera/Getty Images, pp. 3, 14, 21; Mikhail Kniazev/Getty Images, p. 4; Fuse/Getty Images, p. 7; Mr Vito/Getty Images, p. 8; Kobus Louw/Getty Images, p. 10; wavebreakmedia/Shutterstock, p. 12; Os Tartarouchos/Getty Images, p. 14; Ridofranz/Getty Images, p. 16; Tyler Olson/Shutterstock, p. 18. Design element: Agunar/Shutterstock.

Cover: Shawn and Sally Weimer/Getty Images.

Index

To Faisal—always keep reading!

Lerner Publications Company
An imprint of Lerner Publishing Group, Inc.
241 First Avenue North
Minneapolis, MN 55401 USA

For reading levels and more information, look up this title at www.lernerbooks.com.

Main body text set in MIkado.
Typeface provided by HvD Fonts.

Designer: Mary Ross **Photo Editor:** Cynthia Zemlicka
Lerner team: Martha Kranes, Sue Marquis

Library of Congress Cataloging-in-Publication Data

Names: Sanderson, Whitney author
Title: First library card with Big Bird / Whitney Sanderson.
Description: Minneapolis : Lerner Publications, [2026] | Series: Sesame Street firsts | Includes bibliographical references and index. | Audience term: juvenile | Audience term: Children | Audience: Ages 4–8 | Audience: Grades K–1 | Summary: "Borrowing books from a library is fun! But you need a library card to borrow books. Readers will join Big Bird and more Sesame Street friends in learning about getting your first library card"— Provided by publisher.
Identifiers: LCCN 2024038634 (print) | LCCN 2024038635 (ebook) | ISBN 9798765661079 library binding | ISBN 9798765684856 paperback | ISBN 9798765681015 epub
Subjects: LCSH: Libraries—Juvenile literature | Library circulation and loans—Juvenile literature | Library cards—Juvenile literature
Classification: LCC Z665.5 .S255 2026 (print) | LCC Z665.5 (ebook) | DDC 020–dc23/eng/20250203

LC record available at https://lccn.loc.gov/2024038634
LC ebook record available at https://lccn.loc.gov/2024038635

Manufactured in the United States of America
1-1011812-53662-1/13/2025